A

SERIES OF FIGURES

SHEWING

ALL THE MOTIONS

IN THE

MANUAL AND PLATOON

EXERCISES,

AND

THE DIFFERENT FIRINGS,

ACCORDING TO

HIS MAJESTY'S REGULATIONS.

José Maria de Cobaco
Capm 1839

DRAWN FROM LIFE,

BY MAJOR T. L. MITCHELL.

The Naval & Military Press Ltd

Published by

The Naval & Military Press Ltd

Unit 5 Riverside, Brambleside
Bellbrook Industrial Estate
Uckfield, East Sussex
TN22 1QQ England

Tel: +44 (0)1825 749494

www.naval–military-press.com
www.nmarchive.com

*In reprinting in facsimile from the original, any imperfections are inevitably reproduced
and the quality may fall short of modern type and cartographic standards.*

TO THE

ADJUTANT-GENERAL OF THE FORCES,

THESE SKETCHES

ARE, WITH PERMISSION, DEDICATED,

BY

HIS MOST OBLIGED, AND MOST FAITHFUL SERVANT,

T. L. MITCHELL.

LONDON, 25*th September*, 1825.

CONTENTS.

THE MANUAL EXERCISE.

Page in the
Manual and
Platoon Book
referred to.

PLATE.

   I. 1. Secure Arms. *Three Motions* 5

  II. 2. Shoulder Arms. (*From* Secure Arms.) *Three Motions* 6

 III. 3. Order Arms. (*From* Shouldered Arms.) *Three Motions* 6

 IV. 4. Fix Bayonets. *Two Motions* 7

  V. 5. Shoulder Arms. (*From* Fix Bayonets.) *Two Motions* 7

 VI. 6. Present Arms. *Three Motions* 8

 VII. 7. Shoulder Arms. (*From* Presented Arms.) *Two Motions* 9

VIII. 8. Port Arms 9

     9. Charge Bayonets 10

 IX. 10. Shoulder Arms. (*From* Charge Bayonets.) *Two Motions* 10

  X. 11. Advance Arms. (*From* Shouldered Arms.) *Four Motions* 11

 XI. 12. Order Arms. (*From* Advanced Arms.) *Three Motions* 12

 XII. 13. Advance Arms. (*From* Ordered Arms.) *Two Motions* 12

XIII. 14. Shoulder Arms. (*From* Advanced Arms.) *Three Motions* 13

XIV. 15. Support Arms. *Three Motions* 13

    16. Stand at Ease 13

 XV. 17. Attention. 14

    18. Carry Arms. *Three Motions* 14

XVI. 19. Slope Arms 14

    20. Stand at Ease 15

XVII. 21. Attention 15

    22. Carry Arms. (*From* Sloped Arms.) *Two Motions* . . 15

XVIII. 23. Order Arms. (*From* Carried Arms.) *Three Motions* . 15

XIX. 24. Unfix Bayonets 16

    25. Stand at Ease 16

THE

PLATOON EXERCISE

AND

DIFFERENT FIRINGS.

		Page in the Manual and Platoon Book referred to.
PLATE.		
XX.	As front Rank, Prime and Load. *Two Motions*	28
	Handle Cartridge. *Two Motions* . . .	29
XXI.	Prime. *Three Motions*	29
	'Bout. *Three Motions*	29

N.B. In this position, after firing as centre and as rear rank, the butt is brought *inside* the foot.

XXII.	Draw Ramrods. *Two Motions*	30
	Ram down Cartridge. *Four Motions* . .	31
XXIII.	Return Ramrods. *Two Motions*	32
	As front Rank Standing, Ready	32
	P'sent, Fire	32
	(or) Half-cock Arms . .	33
XXIV.	Intermediate Motion before coming to the "shoulder" after Firing, in each Rank	33
	Shoulder Arms	34
	As centre Rank, Ready	34
	As rear Rank Standing, Ready	35
	P'sent, Fire	35
XXV.	As front Rank Kneeling, Ready	36
	As rear Rank Kneeling, Ready	37
	Trail Arms, (" *The long trail*")	42
XXVI.	Prepare to resist Cavalry, Ready	48

EXPLANATION.

THE Figures are numbered in the order of the New Regulations for the Manual and Platoon Exercises.

The Intermediate Motions are represented in Outline; the Perfect Position by a Finished Figure.

The Numbers *under* the Figures mark the Time of each Motion, several Figures being given to illustrate those Motions which consist of distinct Parts.

The interval of Time between each Motion being Two Pauses of the Slow Time of March (equal to 1″ 36″), the Eye is supposed to rest, during that Space only, on the Figure or Figures representing each Motion.

1st. SECURE ARMS!

1   2   3

2.ⁿᵈ SHOULDER ARMS!

1   2   3

Pl. III.

3.ᵈ ORDER ARMS!

1   2   3

4ᵗʰ FIX BAYONETS!

1   2

Pl. V.

5.thSHOULDER ARMS!

1

2

6.th PRESENT ARMS!

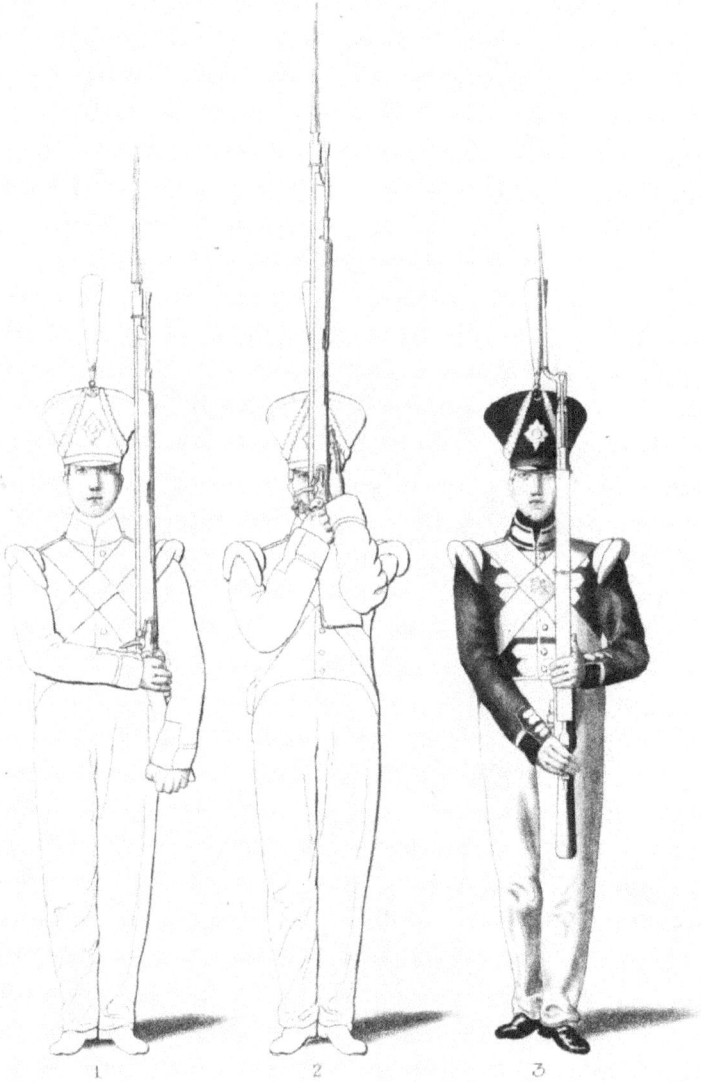

1

2

3

1   2

Pl. VIII.

8.th PORT ARMS!   9.th CHARGE BAYONETS!

Pl. IX.

IDth SHOULDER ARMS!

1   2

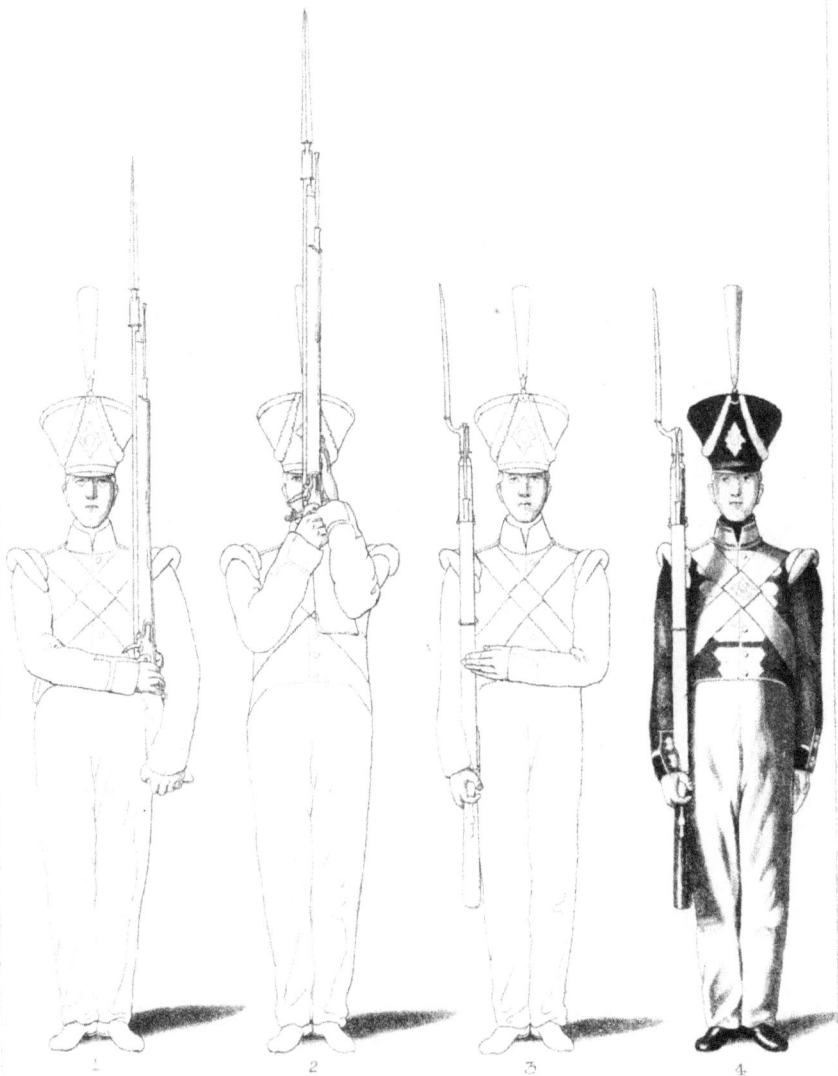

Pl. X.

11th ADVANCE ARMS!

Pl. XI.

12.th ORDER ARMS!

1   2   3

Pl. XII

13.th ADVANCE ARMS!

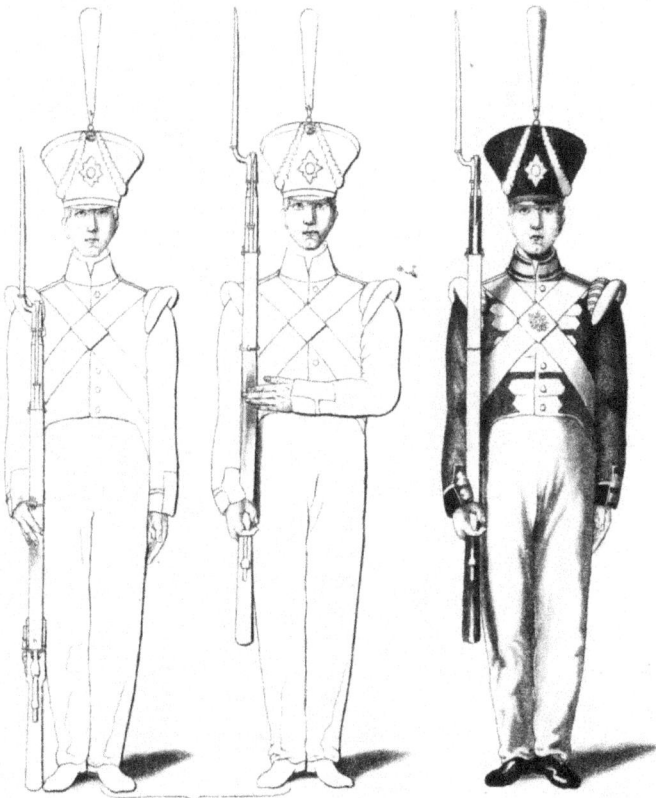

1   2

Pl. XIII.

14.ᵗʰ SHOULDER ARMS!

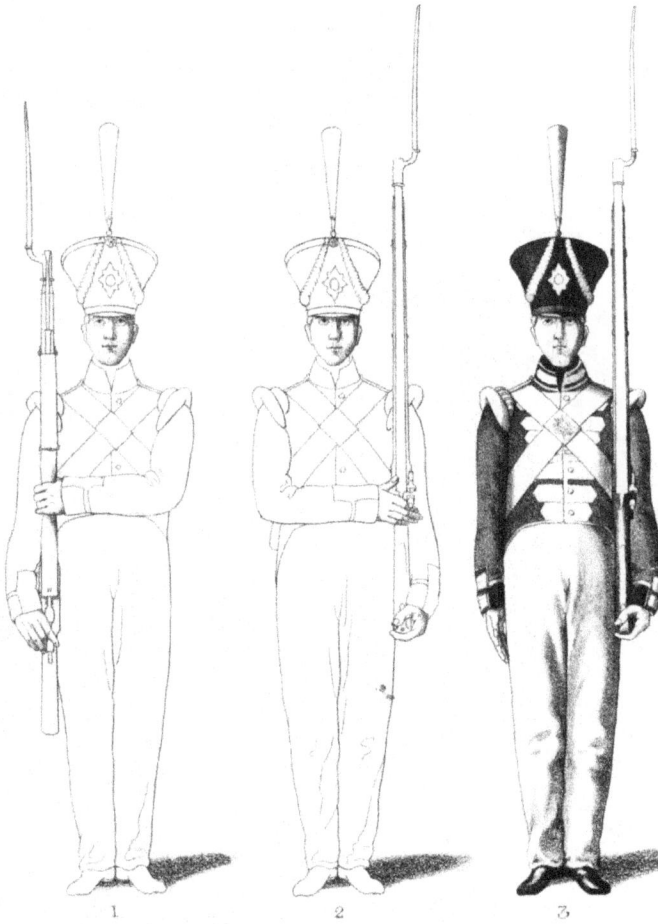

1   2   3

Pl. XIV.

15.th SUPPORT ARMS!   16.th STAND AT EASE!

1   2   3

PL.XV

17th ATTENTION!   18th CARRY ARMS!

1   2   3

Pl. 17.

19.th SLOPE ARMS! 20.th STAND AT EASE!

Pl. 17.

19.th SLOPE ARMS!   20.th STAND AT EASE!

Pl XVII

21ˢᵗ. ATTENTION!   22ⁿᵈ. CARRY ARMS!

1

1   2

Pl. XVIII.

23rd. ORDER ARMS!

1 2 3

PLATE XV.

24th UNFIX BAYONETS!

25th STAND AT EASE!

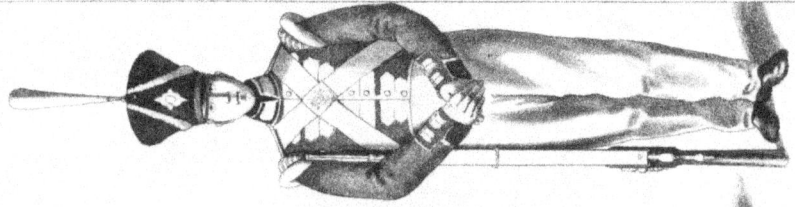

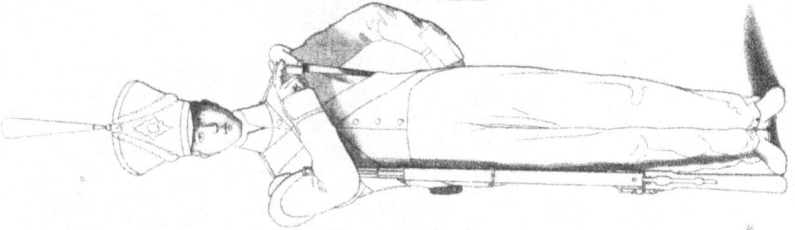

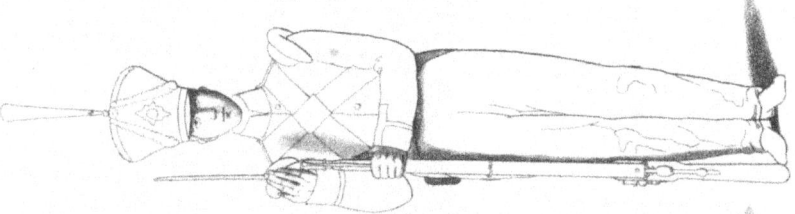

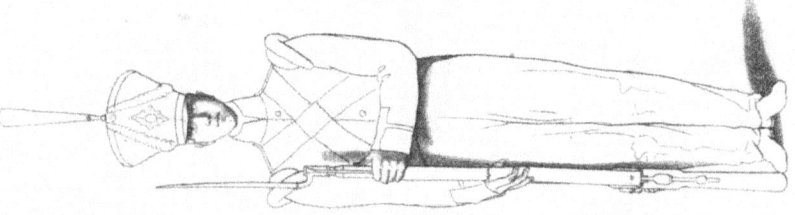

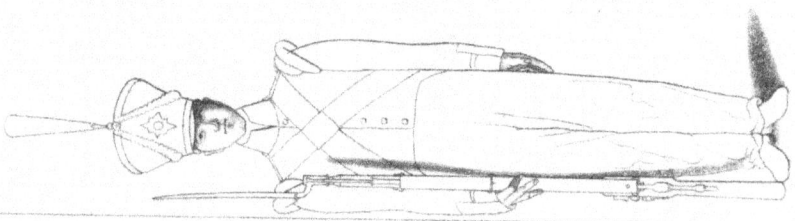

PLATOON EXERCISE

<small>AND</small>

DIFFERENT FIRINGS.

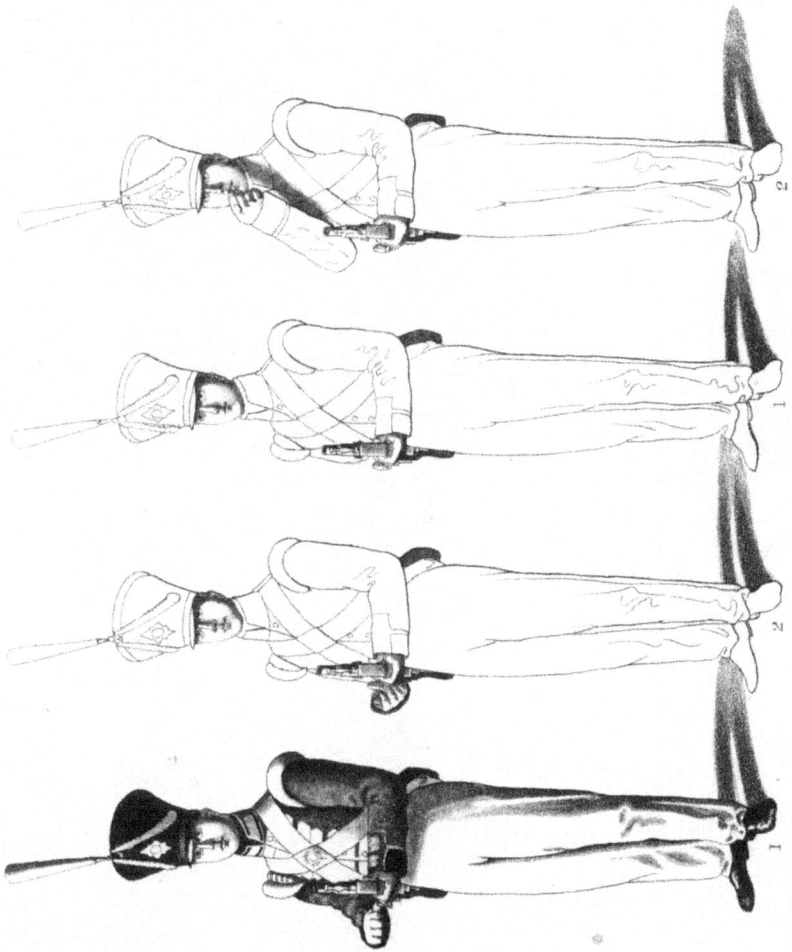

PLATOON EXERCISE.

AS FRONT RANK, PRIME AND LOAD!   HANDLE CARTRIDGE!

PLATE VII.

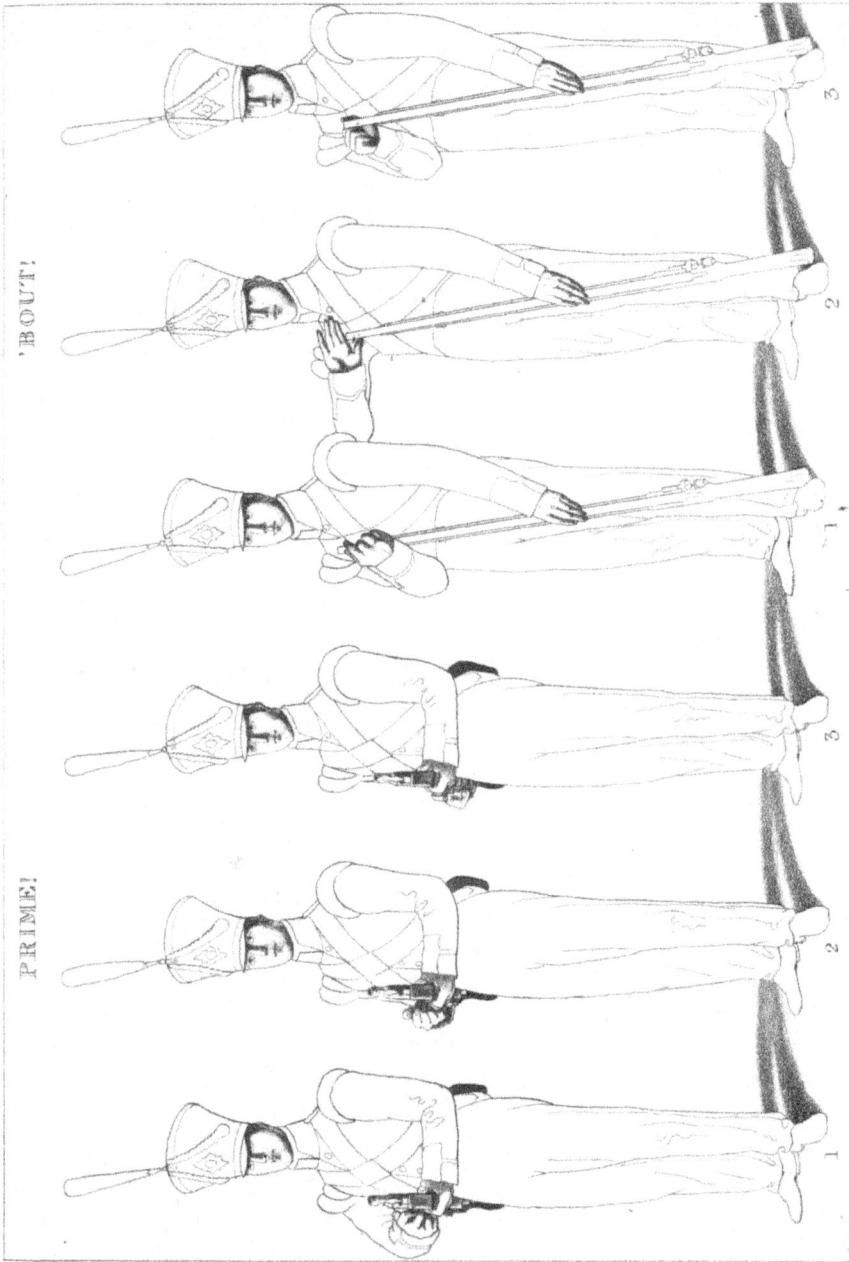

'BOUT!

PRIME!

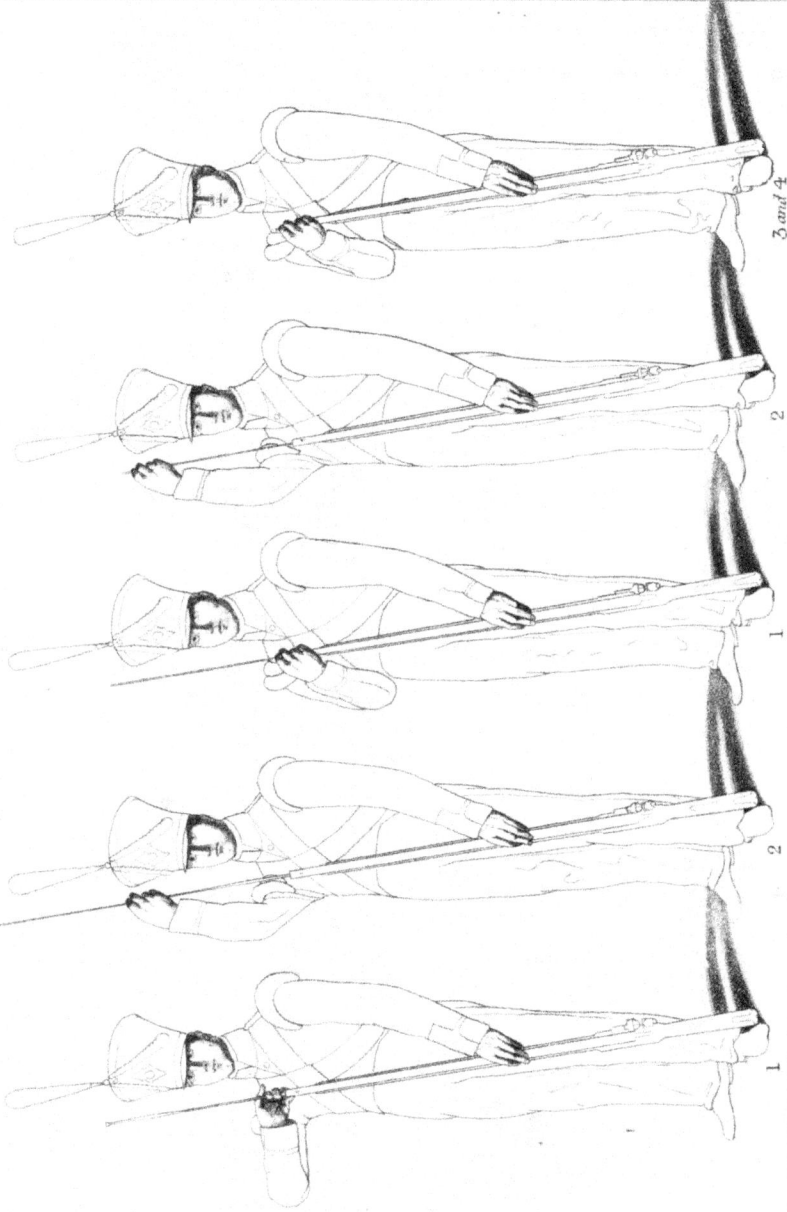

DRAW RAMRODS!

RAM DOWN CARTRIDGE!

PLATE

1

2

1

2

3 and 4

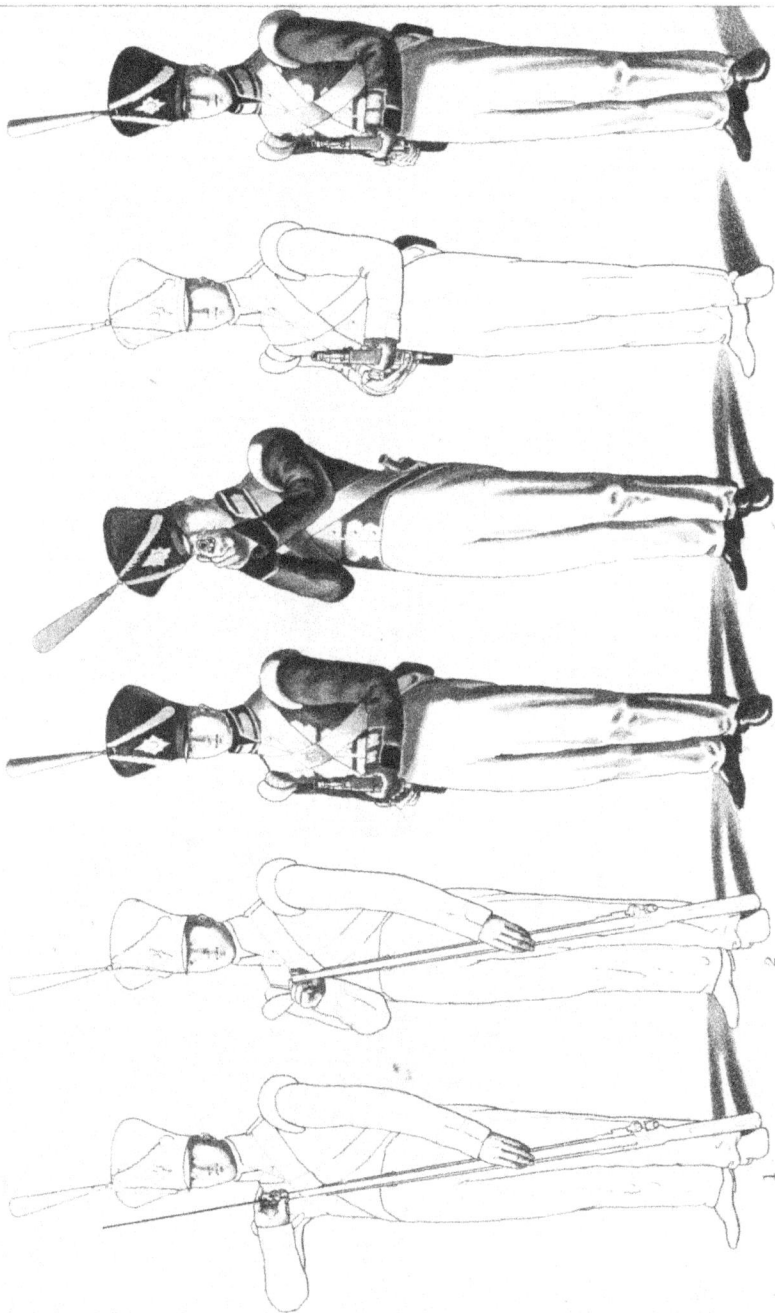

RETURN RAMRODS! READY! P'SENT! FIRE! OR HALF COCK ARMS!

front rank standing

1   2

Pl. XXIX.

SHOULDER ARMS!   READY!   P'SENT FIRE!

Intermediate motion before coming
to the shoulder after firing in each rank.

As centre rank

As rear rank standing

READY!

TRAIL ARMS!

As front rank kneeling.

As rear rank kneeling.

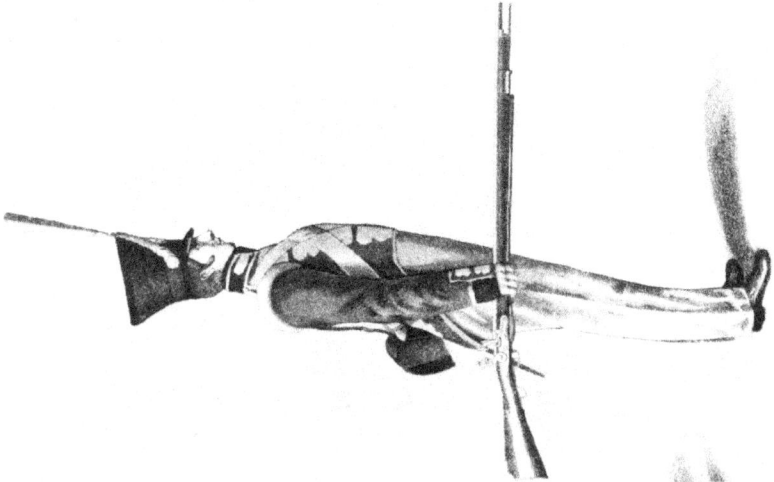

PREPARE TO RESIST CAVALRY. READY!

www.ingramcontent.com/pod-product-compliance
Lightning Source LLC
La Vergne TN
LVHW051803080426
835511LV00018B/3399